D1505745

SECRETS
OF THE
ANIMAL WORLD

FROGS
Living in Two Worlds

by Andreu Llamas
Illustrated by Gabriel Casadevall and Ali Garousi

NARAMATA ELEMENTARY SCHOOL

Gareth Stevens Publishing
MILWAUKEE

For a free color catalog describing Gareth Stevens' list of high-quality books and multimedia programs, call 1-800-542-2595 (USA) or 1-800-461-9120 (Canada). Gareth Stevens Publishing's Fax: (414) 225-0377. See our catalog, too, on the World Wide Web: http://gsinc.com

The editor would like to extend special thanks to Jan W. Rafert, Curator of Primates and Small Mammals, Milwaukee County Zoo, Milwaukee, Wisconsin, for his kind and professional help with the information in this book.

Library of Congress Cataloging-in-Publication Data

Llamas, Andreu.
    [Rana. English]
    Frogs: living in two worlds / by Andreu Llamas ; illustrated by Gabriel Casadevall and Ali Garousi.
        p. cm. – (Secrets of the animal world)
    Includes bibliographical references and index.
    Summary: Describes the physical characteristics, habitat, behavior, and life cycle of frogs.
    ISBN 0-8368-1641-2 (lib. bdg.)
    1. Frogs–Juvenile literature. [1. Frogs.] I. Casadevall, Gabriel, ill. II. Garousi, Ali, ill.
III. Title. IV. Series.
    QL668.E2L65413 1997
    597.8'9–dc21   96-45106

This North American edition first published in 1997 by
Gareth Stevens Publishing
1555 North RiverCenter Drive, Suite 201
Milwaukee, Wisconsin 53212 USA

This U.S. edition © 1997 by Gareth Stevens, Inc. Created with original © 1993 Ediciones Este, S.A., Barcelona, Spain. Additional end matter © 1997 by Gareth Stevens, Inc.

Series editor: Patricia Lantier-Sampon
Editorial assistants: Diane Laska, Rita Reitci

Printed in the United States of America

1 2 3 4 5 6 7 8 9 01 00 99 98 97

CONTENTS

THE WORLD OF THE FROG

Where frogs live

Frogs and toads first appeared almost 200 million years ago. Since then, they have evolved into 24 families and more than 3,800 species, many of which are now extinct.

Frogs can be found all over the world except in Antarctica. They have adapted to a great variety of environments and exist in woods, flat lands, wet zones, and deserts. Some species even live in the Andes and the Himalaya mountains.

The frog's size varies from .4 inches (1 centimeter) to more than 8 inches (20 cm).

Although most species prefer wet, humid areas, frogs exist almost all over the world.

Living on land

The frog is an amphibian, one of a group of animals that moved from life in water to life on land almost 370 million years ago. The word *amphibian* means "a double life" and describes the frog's ability to live in two very different worlds: water and land.

After hatching from eggs, frog larvae are adapted to live in water only. But after metamorphosis, the adult frogs have characteristics that allow them to live on land.

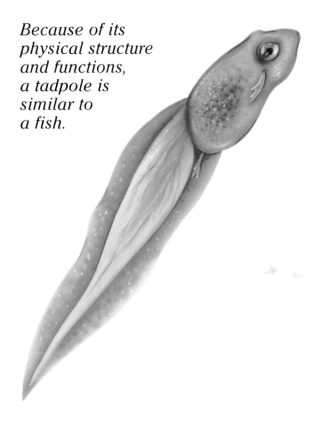

Because of its physical structure and functions, a tadpole is similar to a fish.

After metamorphosis, the adult frog can live out of the water.

Types of amphibians

There are about 3,000 species of amphibians, which can be classified into three living scientific groups, or orders.

The first order, Caudata (or Urodela), includes some 300 species of salamanders and sirens that live mainly in the temperate zones of Europe and North America. These amphibians have long tails and four short legs. They spend most, if not all, of their time in water. The giant salamander of Japan is the largest amphibian in

SALAMANDER
(Caudata)

SAINT ANTHONY FROG
(Anura)

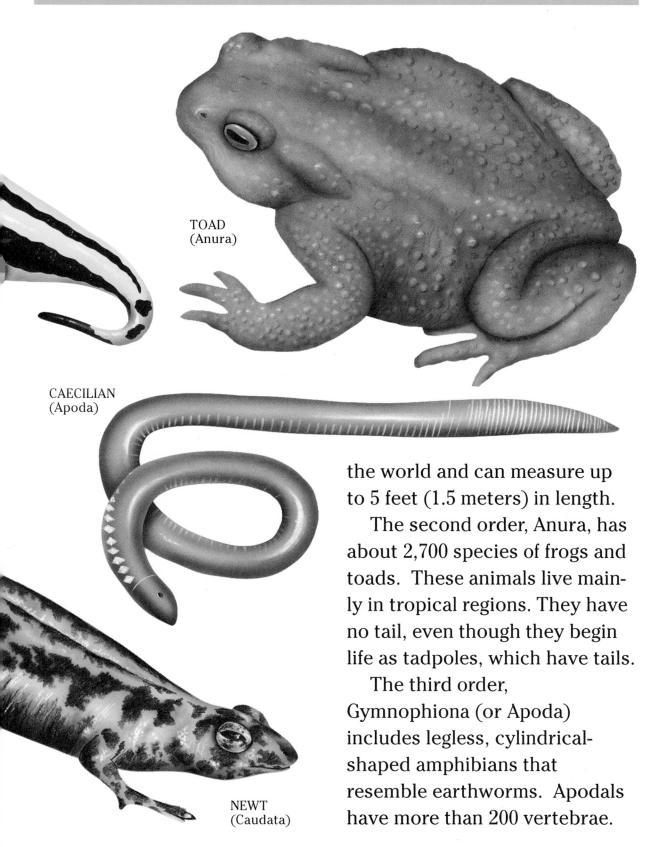

TOAD
(Anura)

CAECILIAN
(Apoda)

NEWT
(Caudata)

the world and can measure up to 5 feet (1.5 meters) in length.

The second order, Anura, has about 2,700 species of frogs and toads. These animals live mainly in tropical regions. They have no tail, even though they begin life as tadpoles, which have tails.

The third order, Gymnophiona (or Apoda) includes legless, cylindrical-shaped amphibians that resemble earthworms. Apodals have more than 200 vertebrae.

INSIDE THE FROG

If you walk along the banks of a river during spring or summer, you will almost certainly hear the sounds of frogs as they jump into the river to escape. By approaching carefully, you might catch a glimpse of them sitting on the bank, quietly waiting for a chance to catch a meal. Frogs have a short, compact body joined to a large head. They have no neck or tail.

SKIN RESPIRATION
Although it has lungs, the frog can also breathe through its skin.

SKIN
The frog regularly sheds its skin and grows new skin.

VERTEBRAL COLUMN

KIDNEYS

PELVIC GIRDLE

UROSTYLE

MUCOUS GLANDS
These glands cover the entire body and produce a secretion that covers the skin to keep it from drying out.

POISON GLANDS
Some frogs have glands in the skin that secrete fluids which can irritate or even kill enemies.

ANUS

FEMUR

ASTRAGÁLUS

CALCANEUS

INTESTINE
During the tadpole stage, the intestine is very long. After metamorphosis, however, it is shorter and simpler.

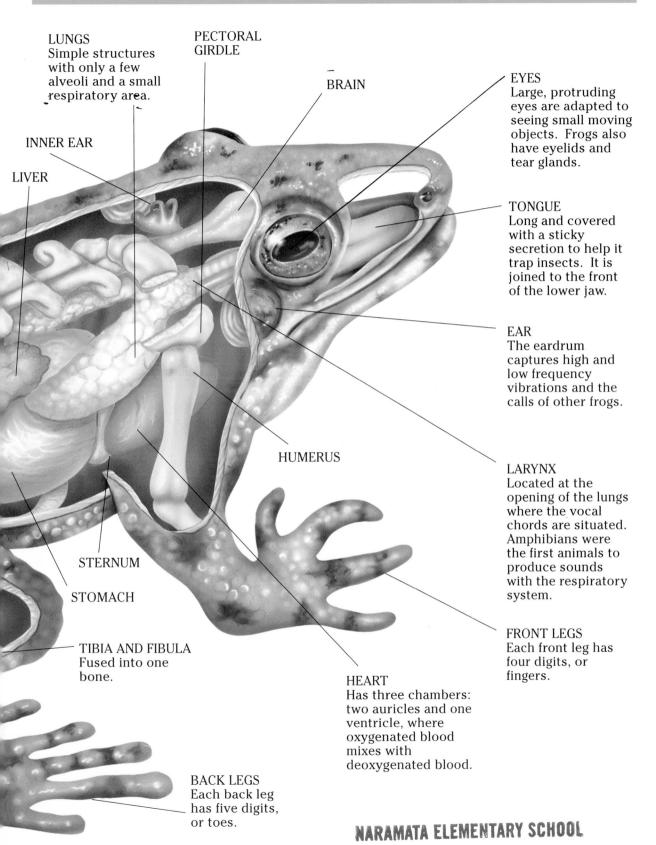

LUNGS
Simple structures with only a few alveoli and a small respiratory area.

PECTORAL GIRDLE

BRAIN

EYES
Large, protruding eyes are adapted to seeing small moving objects. Frogs also have eyelids and tear glands.

INNER EAR

LIVER

TONGUE
Long and covered with a sticky secretion to help it trap insects. It is joined to the front of the lower jaw.

EAR
The eardrum captures high and low frequency vibrations and the calls of other frogs.

HUMERUS

LARYNX
Located at the opening of the lungs where the vocal chords are situated. Amphibians were the first animals to produce sounds with the respiratory system.

STERNUM

STOMACH

FRONT LEGS
Each front leg has four digits, or fingers.

TIBIA AND FIBULA
Fused into one bone.

HEART
Has three chambers: two auricles and one ventricle, where oxygenated blood mixes with deoxygenated blood.

BACK LEGS
Each back leg has five digits, or toes.

THE FROG'S METAMORPHOSIS

Laying thousands of eggs

During the mating season, frogs gather in large groups to mate and reproduce. The males are the first to arrive. They begin singing by swelling the pouches in their throats. When a female comes near, a male quickly climbs on her back, clasps with his front legs, and remains there until the mating is complete. This position is called amplexus. Amplexus is a strong instinctive action by males during the mating period.

Eggs are laid between April and May. There can be as many as ten thousand eggs .04 inch (1 millimeter) thick inside a gelatinous mass. The gelatin

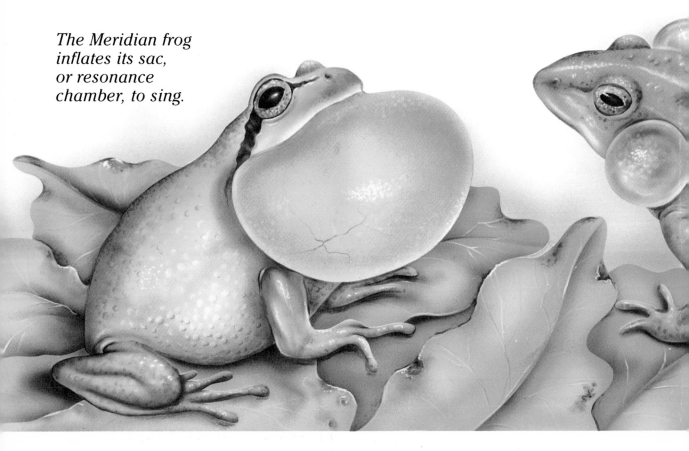

The Meridian frog inflates its sac, or resonance chamber, to sing.

protects the eggs from the elements and from predators. Eggs and gelatin together are called spawn.

Each egg is a small, transparent sphere with a black dot in the center. The eggs are laid in many different patterns, depending on the species.

After a short time, from 5 or 6 days to several weeks, the outer covering of the egg breaks.

The male clings to the first female that is attracted by its song.

This frog has resonance chambers on both sides of its throat.

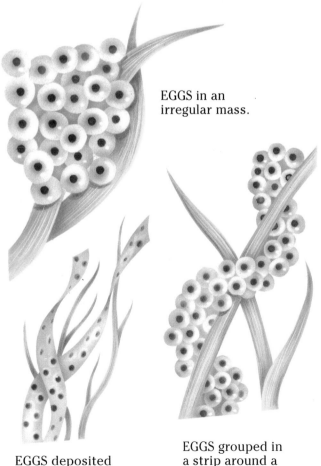

EGGS in an irregular mass.

EGGS deposited in a strand.

EGGS grouped in a strip around a submerged shoot.

A life full of great changes

When a larva comes out of an egg, it stays attached for a while to the egg covering. The mouth is not formed yet, and the larva stays in this position for hours or even days. Gills open on both sides of the larva's head, allowing it to breathe under water. After a few days, a tail grows, the external gills are reabsorbed, and internal gills form. The larva become tadpoles.

After metamorphosis, the eardrums stand out behind the frog's eyes.

The tadpole's mouth is shaped to eat algae.

Recently fertilized EGG.

TADPOLE with a developed tail and external gills.

Back legs appear and the gills become internal.

Front legs appear, and the tail begins to disappear.

The tadpole's mouth has horny teeth that allow it to eat everything, including meat, but it normally eats scrapings from the green weeds that cling to stones on the bottom of the pond. A tadpole will also eat the bodies of any dead animals it finds in the water.

The tadpole remains a tadpole for a few months to a year, depending on the environment and the available food.

The next change — from tadpole to adult frog — is called metamorphosis. The tadpole measures about 1.2 inches (3 cm) in length. The metamorphosis begins with the appearance of back legs, which already have toes. A few days later, the front legs appear.

Several more changes are needed, however, before the adult frog can leave the water and live on land.

ADULT FROG

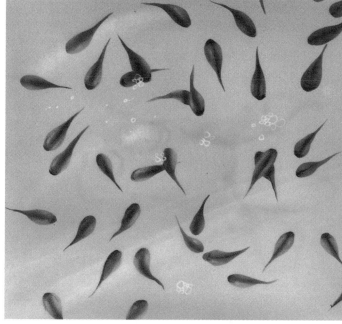

Tadpoles gather in small pools, but many will die if the water dries up.

ADAPTATION TO LIFE OUT OF THE WATER

The last stages of metamorphosis

While the legs are appearing, other changes are happening to the tadpole. The position of its mouth changes, and the gills disappear. It breathes through its lungs, and the tail vanishes. Eventually, the tadpole changes into a small frog, a little more than .4 inch (1 cm) long. In a few months, the metamorphosis is complete, and the frog comes out of the water. During this time, it has started to come to the surface to breathe. It can now live in the open air.

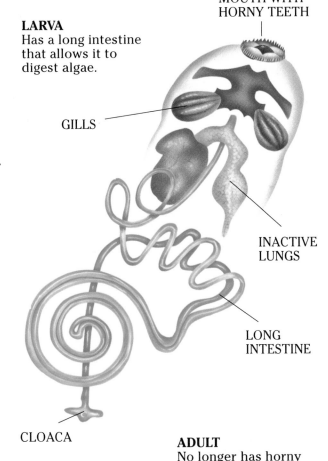

LARVA
Has a long intestine that allows it to digest algae.

MOUTH WITH HORNY TEETH

GILLS

INACTIVE LUNGS

LONG INTESTINE

CLOACA

ADULT
No longer has horny teeth, and the intestine has shortened.

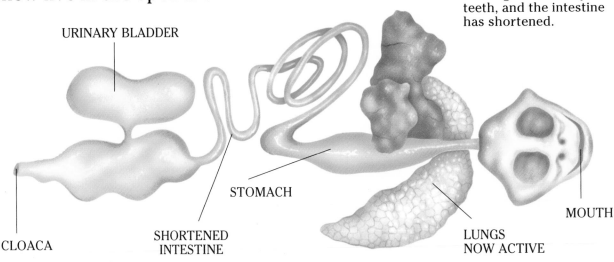

URINARY BLADDER

STOMACH

MOUTH

CLOACA

SHORTENED INTESTINE

LUNGS NOW ACTIVE

that the frog uses its tongue for hunting?

The carnivorous frog has a tongue capable of capturing live prey. It opens its mouth and shoots out its tongue toward a victim. The tongue, which has its own muscles, is joined behind the front end of the lower jaw and folds backward. Covered with a sticky solution, the tongue moves very quickly. It takes the frog less than fifteen-hundredths of a second to capture an insect.

Other methods of reproduction

Many frog species have various ways of protecting their young in the egg and tadpole stages. One of the simplest plans is to stick the eggs onto a leaf or rock near the water. This way, tadpoles fall straight into the water when they hatch from the egg.

Four frog families produce a foam that they wrap around the eggs for protection.

Babies hatching on land.

Hatching fully developed from the egg.

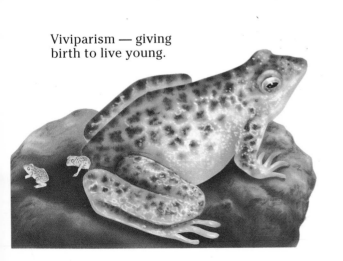

Transporting tadpoles.

Viviparism — giving birth to live young.

Forming a foamy nest.

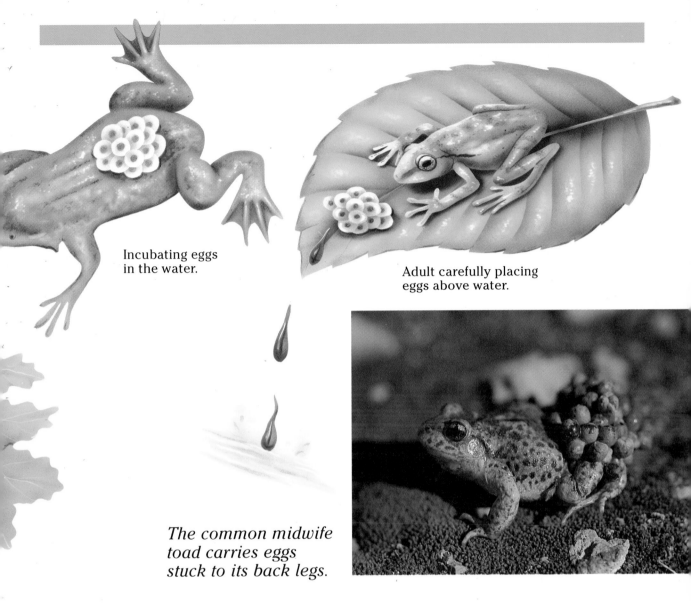

Incubating eggs
in the water.

Adult carefully placing
eggs above water.

*The common midwife
toad carries eggs
stuck to its back legs.*

Nine frog families lay eggs that produce small, fully formed frogs. This is called direct development. Some frog species have a special form of direct development called viviparism. In this case, the female keeps the eggs inside her body until the babies are fully formed. The baby frogs are then born.

In some species, the male or female carries the eggs until they hatch. This way, the parent can easily protect the babies.

The adult male Darwin frog keeps the newly born tadpoles in its mouth sac until they are fully developed. After a few weeks, baby frogs come out of their father's mouth.

ANCESTORS OF THE FROG

The oldest amphibian

The most primitive known amphibian was the Ichthyostega, which lived in Greenland 370 million years ago. It was more than 3.3 feet (1 m) long and had four legs. Each leg had five toes that kept it upright on dry land. It still had some characteristics of the fish, such as a large caudal, or tail, fin; but it also had a short neck, a spinal column, and strong ribs.

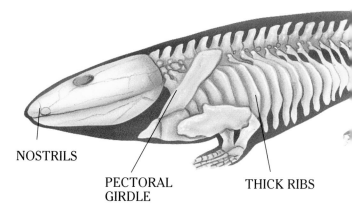

NOSTRILS

PECTORAL GIRDLE

THICK RIBS

Large, primitive Ichthyostega possessed a very strong skeleton.

Because of its shape, the Ichthyostega was quicker in the water than on land. On land, it could only trap prey that moved slowly.

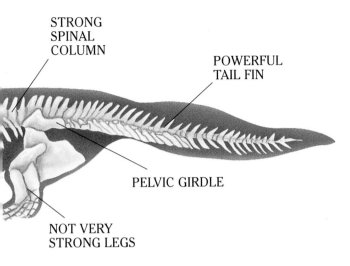

STRONG SPINAL COLUMN

POWERFUL TAIL FIN

PELVIC GIRDLE

NOT VERY STRONG LEGS

Gigantic amphibians

Some amphibians gave up living on land and returned to the water. This resulted in a great increase in their size and weight.

The Mastodonsaurus lived almost 220 million years ago and reached a length of almost 10 feet (3 m). The water helped support the weight of its huge body because its legs were too weak. Its tail, however, was large and strong to help its movement in the water. It spent most of its time hunting for fish.

Mastodonsaurus fossils have been found in Africa and Germany.

that some frogs keep their young in their stomachs?

In one species of Australian frog, the female swallows her eggs and incubates them in her stomach. This is called gastric incubation. To prepare for this, the female stops eating, and her stomach stops producing acid. Incubation takes about six weeks. When the little frogs are ready, they come out of the mother's mouth. Some scientists think this frog may now be extinct.

THE LIFE OF A FROG

A frog's leap

The back legs of a frog are designed to propel the frog through water when swimming, and also for making huge jumps on land. The back legs are specialized for these leaps. When the frog is resting with its legs folded, the bones and muscles are similar to a compressed spring, ready to move forward. This ability is useful for hunting prey and escaping enemies.

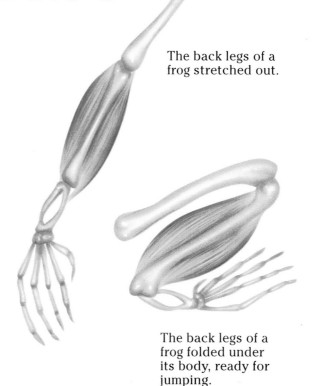

The back legs of a frog stretched out.

The back legs of a frog folded under its body, ready for jumping.

Sequence showing a frog's leap.

Natural enemies

The adult frog is food for many different species of animals, such as foxes and some types of bats.

However, eggs and tadpoles have more enemies than adult frogs because they have no way to defend themselves. In fact, eggs and tadpoles are eaten by insects, fish, reptiles, birds, and mammals. There is also a species of frog that hunts other, smaller types of amphibians, including members of its own species.

Many frog species have camouflage colors. This helps them hide from their enemies.

The bat can distinguish between a poisonous and nonpoisonous frog.

that the frog hunts only moving animals?

The eyes and optic nerves of a frog are adapted so that it attacks and jumps toward any small object that moves, because it thinks the object is an insect.

The frog reacts only when its prey is moving. Without the movement, it is as if the frog sees nothing edible. In addition, some of its optic nerves function as danger detectors. When a shadow falls over the frog's eyes, the nerves send a message to the brain. The frog jumps quickly into the water in case an enemy is near.

APPENDIX TO

SECRETS OF THE ANIMAL WORLD

FROGS
Living in Two Worlds

FROG SECRETS

▼ **Climbing frogs.** On the ends of their digits, Saint Anthony and Meridian frogs have disks that look like suckers. These help them hang on when climbing vertical surfaces. These frogs often climb tree branches or to the tops of bushes.

Cold water frogs. Some frog species live in very cold river water. Females need a longer time to produce eggs, which are laid every two or three years.

Frog fasts. Amphibians can go for a long time, from several months to a year, without eating.

▼ **Flying frog.** The flying frog has long digits on the ends of its feet that are joined to one another by a fine web. It can jump up to 100 feet (30 m), keeping its digits spread to break its fall.

▼ **Colors for all tastes.** The color of a frog's skin depends on the species. Poisonous species, for example, have skin in a variety of very bright colors that warn their enemies of danger.

Fertile frogs. Some frog species, like the bullfrog, can produce between 10,000 and 20,000 eggs a year. But they have a death rate that can reach 99 percent.

Breeding two days a year. Some frog species live in the desert and breed only one or two nights a year, when it rains heavily. The babies grow rapidly, and the tadpole stage may last less than two weeks.

▼ **Fatal poison.** The skin of some frog species in South America secretes a poison. Some tribes of Amazon Indians use this to poison their arrows.

1. Amphibians are made up of:
a) Anura, Caudata, and toads.
b) Anura, amphibians, and Caudata.
c) Anura, Caudata, and Apoda.

2. The oldest known amphibian lived:
a) 170 million years ago.
b) 370 million years ago.
c) 563 million years ago.

3. The change from tadpole to frog is called:
a) amphibian development.
b) amphibian transformation.
c) metamorphosis.

4. The legs of a frog have:
a) 5 front digits and 4 back.
b) 5 front digits and 5 back.
c) 4 front digits and 5 back.

5. The diet of the adult frog is:
a) herbivorous.
b) carnivorous.
c) omnivorous.

6. The male's clasp of the female during mating is called:
a) amplexus.
b) abraplexus.
c) fecundexus.

The answers to FROG SECRETS questions are on page 32.

GLOSSARY

adapt: to make changes or adjustments in order to survive in a changing environment.

algae: a group of plants that grow in water. Algae do not have roots, stems, or leaves.

alveolus (*pl.* alveoli): a tiny air cell of the lung.

amphibians: cold-blooded animals that live both in water and on land. Frogs, toads, and salamanders are amphibians.

camouflage: a way of disguising something or someone to make it look like its surroundings. An animal's camouflage helps it blend in with its habitat, making it more difficult for predators to see.

carnivores: meat-eating animals.

caudal fin: the fin at the top of a fish's tail that adds speed and thrust to the fish's propulsion.

cloaca: a common chamber into which the intestinal, urinary, and genital tracts open.

digit: a finger or toe.

edible: safe to eat; capable of being eaten.

environment: the surroundings in which plants, animals, and other organisms live.

evolve: to change or develop gradually from one form to another. Over time, all living things evolve to survive in their changing environments, or they may become extinct.

external: on the outside or outer surface.

extinct: no longer in existence.

fertilize: to make ready for reproduction, growth, or development.

fossils: the remains of plants or animals from an earlier time period that are often found in rock or in Earth's crust.

gills: the breathing organs in all fish and some other animals; also known as the branchiae.

glands: organs in the body that make and release substances such as sweat, tears, and saliva.

hatch: to break out of an egg.

humid: damp; having a lot of moisture in the air.

incubate: to keep eggs warm, usually with body heat, so they will hatch.

inflate: to fill with air or gas, causing to expand.

instinct: a pattern of activity or a tendency that is inborn.

internal: located within or inside something.

larva (*pl.* larvae): in the life cycle of insects, amphibians, fish, and some other organisms, the stage that comes after the egg but before full development.

mammals: warm-blooded animals that have backbones. Female mammals produce milk to feed their young.

mate (*v*): to join together (animals) to produce young.

metamorphosis: a complete change in form or appearance. Metamorphosis often occurs in various stages.

optic: having to do with the eyes or eyesight.

pouch: a part of the body that is like a bag, or sac.

predators: animals that hunt other animals for food.

prey: animals that are hunted for food by other animals.

primitive: of or relating to an early and usually simple stage of development.

reproduce: to mate, create offspring, and bear young.

respiration: the act of breathing.

sac: a part of a plant or animal that is like a pouch, or bag.

secretion: a substance, usually a liquid, that is produced by a bodily organ.

shed: to lose as part of a natural process; for example, a frog sheds its skin.

sirens: eel-shaped amphibians that have external gills as well as lungs.

spawn: to lay or deposit eggs; the eggs of aquatic animals.

species: animals or plants that are closely related and often similar in behavior and appearance. Members of the same species are capable of breeding with one another.

sphere: a globe-shaped object.

tadpole: a newly-hatched frog or toad that lives in water and has a tail and gills.

temperate: not extreme; relating to climatic zones with warm summers and cold winters that lie between the warm tropics and the cold polar regions.

tropical: belonging to the tropics, or the region centered on the equator and lying between the Tropic of Cancer (23.5 degrees north of the equator) and the Tropic of Capricorn (23.5 degrees south of the equator). This region is typically very hot and humid.

vertebrae: small, interconnected segments of bone that make up the spinal column.

vertical: straight up and down.

ACTIVITIES

◆ Designs of textiles, wallpaper, and other kinds of decoration are often taken from patterns found in nature. Many frogs, especially tree frogs, and salamanders, have beautiful patterns that a designer might want to utilize. Find some books and magazines that contain color pictures of several kinds of frogs and salamanders. Draw a series of 3-inch (1.2-cm) squares on white paper. Then, using crayons, color pencils, or watercolors, copy the pattern of a different frog or salamander in each square. Write the name of the animal next to its pattern. The next time you need a pattern for a project, choose one from your collection of frog and salamander designs.

◆ Frogs benefit humans in many ways. Read more about frogs to answer the following questions. What are some direct ways frogs help humans? What are some indirect ways they help us? Do they have a beneficial effect upon the environment? What impact do frogs have on mosquitoes and other kinds of insects?

MORE BOOKS TO READ

Amazing Frogs and Toads. Barry Clarke (Knopf Books)
The Complete Frog. Elizabeth A. Lacey (Lothrop)
Frog. Michael Chinery (Troll Communications)
The Frog in the Pond. Jennifer Coldrey (Gareth Stevens)
Frogs, Frogs Everywhere. D. M. Souza (Lerner Group)
Frogs and Toads. Bobbie Kalman and Tammy Everts
    (Crabtree Publishing)
Frogs and Toads. Steve Parker (Sierra)
Tadpole to Frog. Oliver S. Owen (Abdo and Daughters)
Tree Frogs. Sylvia A. Johnson (Lerner Group)
Treefrogs. James E. Gerholdt (Abdo and Daughters)

VIDEOS

The Frog. (Encyclopædia Britannica)
Frogs: An Investigation. (Phoenix/BFA Films and Video)
Frogs and How They Live. (AIMS Media)
Frogs and Toads. (Wood Knapp Video)
Frogs, Toads, and Salamanders. (Agency for Instructional Technology)

PLACES TO VISIT

Baltimore Zoo
In Druid Hill Park
Baltimore, MD 21217

Metro Toronto Zoo
Meadowvale Road
West Hill, Ontario M1E 4R5

Adelaide Zoo
Frome Road
Adelaide, South Australia
Australia 5000

St. Louis Zoological Park
In Forest Park
1 Government Drive
St. Louis, MO 63110

**Royal Melbourne
    Zoological Gardens**
Elliott Avenue
Parkville, Victoria
Australia 3052

**Vancouver Public
    Aquarium**
Stanley Park
Vancouver, BC
V6B 3X8

Wellington Zoo
Wellington, New Zealand

INDEX